# It's Hot

**Written by Beth Jenkins Grout**
**Illustrated by John Emil Cymerman**

Modern Curriculum Press
A Division of Simon & Schuster
299 Jefferson Road, P.O. Box 480
Parsippany, NJ 07054 - 0480

Design and production by MKR Design, Inc.


ISBN: 0-8136-2016-3  Modern Curriculum Press


3 4 5 6 7 8 9 10  SP  01 00 99 98 97

Mom, I'm hot.

Do you want a hat?

Do you want a cap?

No, I want a fan.

Mom, I'm hot.

Do you want a can of pop?

Do you want to sit on this rock?

No, I want a fan.

Mom, I'm still hot.

Okay, go get the fan.

I've got the fan.